Struck by Love

Copyright © 2017 Marjorie Sadin
All rights reserved.

Published by Goldfish Press, Seattle
4545 42nd Avenue Southwest
Suite 211
Seattle, Washington, 98116

Manufactured in the United States of America

ISBN 13: 978-0971160187
ISBN 10: 097116018X

Cover & Book Design by Koon Woon

This book was set on the Monotype Book Antiqua

Struck by Love

Poetry of Marjorie Sadin

Goldfish Press
Seattle

Acknowledgements

Thanks to the editors of the following journals in which these poems have previously appeared:

Bewildering Stories
Without Fanfare
Holding the Sky
Without Bees
I Miss Stars
Ocean of Love
Down the Rue De La Paix
Autumn Passion
Dumbfounded
Finding My Way Home

Blaze VOX Press
Pigeons in Union Station
The Ascension of the Sun
Kettering Hall

Door is A Jar Magazine
Aptos, California April, 2017

Eunoia Press
Coffee and Ice Cream

Federal Poets Magazine
Trace
A Butterfly

Gutter Eloquence Press
Some Placed Nice

Ink Sweat and Tears
Six Rowers

Poetry Pacific
Heat Lightning
Caught in Torrent
Summer

Subsync Press
Poem of the Month
How to Live with What You Have

Tower Journal
Anniversary
October

Contents

Dumbfounded / 1
I Miss Stars / 2
Without Bees / 3
Kettering Hall / 4
Coffee and Ice Cream / 6
Six Rowers / 7
Without Fanfare / 8
Down the Rue De La Paix / 9
Aptos, California April 2017 / 10
Ocean of Love / 11
Anniversary / 12
The Ascension of the Sun / 13
Summer / 14
Heat Lightning / 15
Holding the Sky / 16
A Butterfly / 17
How to Live with What You Have / 18
Pigeons in Union Station / 19
Caught in Torrent / 20
Mirror / 21
Descent / 22
Finding My Way Home / 23
Women's March, January 21, 2017 / 24
The News / 25
October / 26
Autumn Passion / 27
Incognito / 28
Some Place Nice / 29
Trace / 30

For Michael

Dumbfounded

A deer pauses, not six feet from me.
It lopes across the street and disappears.
It is wild, but unafraid.

I am wild like the deer
but not afraid to commit to you.

Like the understanding between the sun and the moon,
that take turns rising and setting,
we take turns giving and receiving.

Still I am foolish and shy.
Like the deer, I pause and retreat
into my mind.

When I am near you,
I am a deer frozen in the light
struck by love.

I Miss Stars

I miss the stars
And the salt of the ocean.
I miss the whinnying of horses
And the smell of pine trees.

I miss you
And your scent like the mulch of the earth.
I miss mamma's granola
And the sound of the guitar.

I miss cotton fields
And August in Savannah.
I miss sparks from a fire
And steaks grilled with corn.

I miss childhood.
Was there ever one?
I miss innocence
Cloaked in words.

I miss parades
And peace rallies.
I miss promises
And pacts between pals.

I miss the stars
Orion, the Crab Nebula, the Big Dipper.
I miss long nights
And waking to touch.

Without Bees

The stars rain.
They pollinate, too.
Bees also.
One stung me as a child.

When momma died the stars cried.
I never expected her to die,
stung.

Now the stars hardly rain anymore
And children grow up without bees,
and can't be hurt.

Kettering Hall

Apple blossom petals covering the sidewalks.
Kettering Hall at 6 AM in the morning--
early for my Calculus class. It is still dark.
I am in love with a male dancer named Eli.
I do Tai Chi and hope to see him between classes.

I take creative writing classes and write one poem about Eli.
I take long walks in the woods alone. I miss home,
eat in the Natural Foods dining room next to a boy
with long blond hair who gets ten page letters from
his girlfriend.
He slits his wrists.

Eli has many girlfriends. I am just one.
He has dark curly hair and a slender physique.
I play old Joni Mitchell records
and sing along with them.
For my birthday, I imagine
a surprise party. I go home instead,
smitten with Eli.

When I get home, I do Tai Chi in the living room,
and I talk incessantly about Eli.
I start smoking Marlboro cigarettes.
I write three letters to Eli and he returns one at the
end of the summer-
"A letter to a letter from. Maybe I needed some
 kind of help?" He signs it
"L, Eli."

But now I wake early to apple blossoms on my walk
and I wait for you to wake up.
We hold hands on the couch and make love
in the afternoons and love is something very
different from what I imagined those mornings in
Kettering Hall.

Now it is just you and I and I don't have to be
drunk or unhinged to say I love you.
I don't do Tai Chi anymore,
but you are in my life, and petals still cover the
sidewalks.

Coffee and Ice Cream

We greet the morning,
coffee and ice cream for breakfast.

The stream flows east toward the river.
The eddies from the stream are like shaving cream.

I dip my feet in the stream.
I kiss your cheeks.

When the sun sets its red curtains,
I am overcome.

I follow you to the shadow of the moon
where there is no light.

Six Rowers

Six rowers on the river in mid-spring,
with a motor boat and a man with a megaphone
preaching to the rowers.

The six rowers go under a bridge.
I can barely see them.
And I am inside the tiny boat in my mind's eye,
rowing furiously.

As if I could stay alive
merely by rowing,
I dream of a cold river
and being on that river.
Rowing, rowing rowing.

Without Fanfare

Without all the fanfare, I love you.
I hover over you like fog.
Don't be afraid, the moon is descending.
The mountains turn into witnesses.

Without further ado, I love you.
I don't put on any airs.
The moon is descending
I make valleys out of mountains,
and mountains of love.

I love you without thinking.
It's like getting dressed in the morning.
The moon is descending
And I hover over you like dawn.
The mountains blush, the valleys are breathless…

Down the Rue De La Paix

Down the Rue de la Paix, peaceful street, was our hotel.
Shootings and bombings dominated the news.

We followed the crooked streets to the Picasso Museum
and to Pere Lachaise Cemetery
almost hearing Chopin's preludes.

The St. Sulpice and Notre Dame stood solemn
with stained glass and organ music.
The wine, the bread, the Parisians pleasured us.

We made love in Paris,
never to return.

Aptos, California April 2017

The ocean drum rolls onto the shore.
Seagulls syncopate. Pipers pluck the sand helter skelter.

Following Route 1 South to an overlook on Point Lobos
where the ocean sprays onto the rock and then recedes.

The waves turn back on themselves
into the ocean the way you return to me.

Where does the ocean end and the horizon begin?
Where do you end and I begin?

Ocean of Love

Remember the fog horn and the lighthouse?
Fathomless depths?

Adrift, I navigate the dark.
My heart cargo headed for shore.

Remember going too far?
Where is the lighthouse?

My heart a fog horn.
Underneath us,
an ocean of love.

Anniversary

This is the anniversary of your death.
When the forsythias bloom,
I pick one from the garden. Spring is a time of renewal,
my birthday and the anniversary of your death.

I'd have done it differently.
You kept asking does he love me? Do I love him?
And I wanted to promise you it was forever.
Everything dies. You never told me that.

There is the promise of summer in the air. Magnolias
blossom. Cherry trees. An awkward truth, sometimes it gets
so hot I can barely breathe. You stopped breathing.

The cicadas will be back this year. You return
in my dreams. I could have done it differently.
Loved you more, him less.

The Ascension of the Sun

Fir trees lift their arms in Hosannas.
Mountains and valleys misty eyed break
into dawn.

I take for granted the flowers and the leaves.
I trample on dreams.
Still the dawn eyes me.

What am I here for?
A movie screen encounter?
A kiss or a shrug?

When I awaken, the sun rubs its eyes.
The wind sweeps the grasses.
I am alone.

Morning is a dress rehearsal.
I forget my lines.

Evergreens rise.
The sun begins its long ascent.
I am an afterthought.

Summer

Summer is fraught with desire
like burrs that cling to your socks.

I grow up a weed,
become characters I could never hope to be
like Lara or the French Lieutenant's Woman.

My best friend fills me in about sex. My hand trembles
when I get a crush.

Heat Lightning

I was a child with a child's awe.
I will be old and dying.

As a child, August heat lightning was like a bonfire
in the sky.
Old age will be like coals glowing after a fire.

Death pours water on my consuming life.

Desire could come suddenly
like a downpour of rain,
linger like a wet wash cloth.

When love dies, the survivors
are outraged.

Holding the Sky

My anger bellows.
Showers pound the ground.

And then it ends.
Gone.

Why on you?
Because you're in reach.

You flash like lightning
after my rage.
My thunder may frighten.
Not you.

You bend,
take me in your arms
the way a rainbow holds the sky.

A Butterfly

A butterfly alights on my blouse
I flick it off.
So easy to say "no".

A hummingbird hovers over the flower.
Staying in the moment, it meditates.
Then moves on.

The weeds uproot the flowers.
You are a weed.
I pluck you.

The river speaks Yiddish.
It smells like a river.
Sometimes it dances.

So easy to say "no".
The river and the trees
discard their leaves.

A butterfly alights on my blouse.
It likes me!
But I flick it off like the ashes of my cigarette.

How to Live With What You Have

Throw out torn socks.
Save scratch paper.
Meet friends for coffee.
Make love on the creaky bed.

Pick up the dog's shit.
Hand wash dishes.
Watch TV without cable.
Use a cell phone without texting.

Use the metro instead of driving.
Travel light.
Let the dicey heavens win the lottery.
Die penniless writing poetry

Go nowhere.
And always be near.

Pigeons in Union Station

Inside the railroad terminal, pigeons bob their heads.
You and I have hot pretzels and coke in the food court.
Over twenty years, we've been friends.
I met you when we were both on Thorazine
Overweight and spaced out.
When I told you my diagnoses you were bowled over —
It was the same as yours!
When I OD'd on Klonopin- you visited me every day in the psych ward.
And brought flowers and food.
You and I are now different people.
We love to watch the pigeons strut and bob
Even though they are trapped in Union Station
The way we were.

Caught in Torrent

The river quivers.
Before the storm, I am wary as a worm.
I have been here before.
The wind is gentle as a girl's skirt,
still and ominous. There is a moment
when I am no longer me.

The morning gift wraps the sun in haze.
Then there is a sprinkle of rain
like the spray from the bow of a boat.
I am anxious the storm will follow.
What am I afraid of? Next the rain will be
like Chinese ink brush on water.

The river stirs, a green leviathan.
Afterwards, my feet are soaked.

Mirror

The river is a mirror
It's moving!
A gull is on top of a log
that floats.

Nothing is new.

The sun leaves its footprints
on the water
and chases away clouds.

Cirrus, Cumulous
run for their lives.

And I am looking for myself
in the breeze of the evergreens
lining the shore.

And I don't see myself—
just the melodrama of the waves,
hissing and praising the sky.

Descent

Darkness descends on the city.
Lights glimmer. A pared moon shines.

I am in a bus headed nowhere. How will I get back?
I want my mother, but she is dead.

I wake, remember that I saw my mother.
I dreamt she was trying to tell me how much
she loved me.

I have a boyfriend who reads while I am sleeping.
I dream of him as an apparition. He turns into my
father who scolds me for the dust in my apartment.
I am afraid my father will die soon.

At college I burn candles on my bed.
They kick me out, and I end up in a hospital in a city
with no stars.

After I die, I will be blind to the moon and stars
and return in someone else's dream.

Finding My Way Home

I used to tear around alone with no direction
like a spinning top. I imagined lovers and chased
them away. I was dependent on a caress.

Once I did acid and thought the clouds
were a web that was going to break and I would die.
But I found my way home and cried and cried.
.
Freezing rain is predicted.
I am warm and sleepy hibernating in this condo.
I need you like fire needs oxygen.

With you, life is real and when it hurts
I still cry out but you hear me and I am not lost
in a web of illusions.

You hold my homesick heart.

Women's March
January 21, 2017

Together women hold signs "We the People Are Greater Than Fear."
Women with pink pussy hats rebuke a man who brags about sexual assault.

They knit pink hats and they curse as they miss
a stitch, curse the man who would take away
their rights about their own bodies.

Women have a voice. They organize at kitchen tables, at children's playgrounds, at
coffee breaks, online. Tweets reach millions worldwide.

Women speak a common language.

"I'm with her," says one sign. And I'm with the grandmother from Spokane and the lesbians from Michigan…

We rise up like vast fields of wheat.
I feel the rustle shoulder to shoulder.
We have come to break the silence.

The News

Why does knowledge frighten?
These girls might still be doctors, engineers, poets.

"Where is my child? Help me find her."
Does anyone hear?
Act?
Care?

These girls in bondage, me in restraints.
The taste of freedom—juicy and sweet.

A locked ward like a terrorist cell in the jungle,
Like playing hide and seek.

Can a poem find these girls?
I can only imagine.
I can only believe.

October

Trees wear their colors out.
Clouds gather like congregations.
It is Yom Kippur.
I have sinned the sins of omission, of broken promises, of resentment.
I have not killed or committed adultery or stolen.
Long days make way for shorter ones.
Less time to contemplate.
It is dark in the morning when I go for my walk.
When I reach the river, it repents too.
It swallows a reflection of leaves.
It has made a sanctuary for seagulls
above its polluted waters.
In autumn the forest is penitent.
The river beats her breast.
And this Yom Kippur,
I will not fast.

Autumn Passion

The puffed up clouds. The Autumn smell of fire.
Near dusk. Birds rustle in the bushes.
You, out of breath; me, lost in thought.

The sun is descending. Rouge on its lips.

Neither of us prays. But, I still ask
 God to keep you alive.
The sun marries the horizon; they come together
 as one.

The trees change colors. Orange, red, yellow.
They undress in winter.
We consummate our autumn flame.

Incognito

It's freezing here. After I do the wash,
I want to smoke a cigarette. But I don't
smoke anymore.

I check books out of the library.
And don't read them. I subscribe to *Time* magazine
and use the articles to light the fire.

I lost 40 pounds, date online.

I am shopping
for your profile.

When you find me,
I will make you cry.

Some Place Nice

You don't ask why.
You just do what God says.
And when He's through with you,
OK so He sends you some place nice,
that is
six feet under His flowers.

Trace

Rain and clouds give way to snow —
and we're only in October.
Days seem to fly by like Frisbees.
One minute I'm 16 and getting high. The next I'm retired.
And in-between, I don't recall.

How do birds keep warm in winter? The radiator groans.
There is no sun today — it has called in absent.
I am growing old, yes, and it is growing colder.

It is a wintry mix. The TV has weather maps.
A cold front and more snow predicted.
The clouds follow me like disciples.
I can't escape the insistent ticking of this storm.

The snow marks time. It doesn't stick. When I go, I'll leave no trace
that I have ever been.

www.ingramcontent.com/pod-product-compliance
Lightning Source LLC
Chambersburg PA
CBHW022349040426
42449CB00006B/789